LOVELINES

Notes from Spirit
on Loving and
Being Loved

....

As told through **JOHN MᶜKIBBIN**
to **GATES MᶜKIBBIN**

LIFELINES LIBRARY

For information, contact:

Field Flowers, Inc.
641 Healdsburg Avenue
Healdsburg, CA 95448
707 433 9771
www.fieldflowers.com
www.lifelineslibrary.com

Cover and text design by Kajun Design

Front cover detail from "Emilie Flöge"
by Gustav Klimt (Erich Lessing/Art Resource)

Author's photo by Christina Schmidhofer

ISBN 1-929799-01-2

 Printed with soy-based ink on recycled paper,
30% post-consumer

*To my mother and best friend, Alice Gates
McKibbin, whose unconditional love is an
unwavering beacon in my life, and to my sister
Nancy Neuhalfen and my brothers John, Philip
and David McKibbin, whose spunky, steadfast
love gives meaning to the word "family"*

What began three years ago as a series of journal entries is now coming into the world as a series of books. All along the way people with the perspective and expertise I needed crossed my path at exactly the right time. Each person has contributed soul and substance to the project. I am abundantly grateful to:

- ♦ **Ned Engle**, who saw what my writings could become long before I did and then adroitly guided me there.
- ♦ **Barbra Dillenger, Michael Makay, Benjo Masilungan** and **Anthony Corso**, whose comments on each new manuscript reassured me of the accuracy and usefulness of the material.
- ♦ **Judith Appelbaum** and **Florence Janovic** at Sensible Solutions, whose savvy counsel about the publishing industry kept me confident and on course.
- ♦ **Carol Fall**, who offered discerning marketing advice and was the creative force behind the book titles.
- ♦ **Erin Blackwell** and **Cynthia Rubin**, whose editorial finesse honored and strengthened the messages.
- ♦ **Laurie Smith** and **Pat Koren** at Kajun Design, who transformed each book into a jewel within and without.

Also by Gates McKibbin:

The Light in the Living Room: Dad's Messages from the Other Side

A Course in Courage: Disarming the Darkness with Strength of Heart

A Handbook on Hope: Fusing Optimism and Action

The Life of the Soul: The Path of Spirit in Your Lifetimes

Available Wisdom: Insights from Beyond the Third Dimension

CONTENTS

GLOSSARY

Creation consists of multiple dimensions of reality. Each dimension is characterized by its vibratory or magnetic quality. The higher the frequency at which the dimension vibrates, the more at one it is with God. The **higher realms** are the dimensions of spiritual reality beyond the material world, where distinctions based on time and space do not exist.

Karma is composed of imprints on your soul created by your choices (thoughts, words and actions). Choices that embrace spirit heal, balance, complete and remove karmic imprints from your current and prior lifetimes that distance your soul from God. Choices that deny or avoid spirit add new imprints that must be healed, balanced, completed and removed later.

Your **lesson** is the larger karmic pattern or theme you are addressing during this lifetime.

Your **mission** is the major contribution you are making in this lifetime to enable the evolution of collective consciousness toward oneness with God.

Your **soul** is the vessel for your spirit. It carries an

infinite variety of karmic imprints that record the experiences your spirit has had, in and out of embodiment. Your soul is all love and light. It represents your limitless potential to embrace spirit to the fullest capacity.

Spirit guides are spiritual entities who have committed to helping you follow the path of love and contribute to the spiritual evolution of all creation. They whisper in your ear telepathically. They send you insights and intuitive flashes. They reaffirm your deepest inner knowing that there is a benevolent higher power inherent in all things.

The **third dimension** is the material reality on planet earth. It consists of dense physical matter that vibrates slowly. The third dimension is characterized by segmented linear time (past, present and future) and compartmentalized space (measurements, boundaries and separation).

The **veil** is a magnetic field surrounding planet earth that separates the vibratory capacity of the third dimension from that of the higher realms. It forms a barrier between your earthly awareness and your higher consciousness. The veil creates the illusion that material reality—and your survival in it—is your reason for being.

The term **we** that is used throughout this book refers to John McKibbin, the spirit who was Gates' father in this lifetime, and the other spiritual entities collaborating with him on the messages he sent down to her.

LOVE NOTES

Like all of the other books in the LifeLines Library, this one arrived out of the blue. I had planned to go to Carmel, California for a respite in a spirit-filled home on the beach. My intention was to use the solitude to review one last time the books channeled from my deceased father, John McKibbin, that I was about to publish.

Two days before my departure date, Dad turned the light on in my living room. He does that whenever he wants to get my attention so that I will slow down long enough to hear what he has to say.

When I saw that the light had come on, I grabbed paper and pen and began writing the message Dad was sending me telepathically. He said that there was yet another book for me to bring down from the higher planes, and that it would be on the topic of love. He also mentioned that if I wanted to work on it while I was in Carmel, he and his colleagues from the other side would be available to collaborate with me. Then he began to send down the first messages in the book. I was halfway through the third one when the telephone rang and jarred me out of my connection with him.

I did, in fact, write this entire book during that brief interlude by the sea. I sat in a comfortable chair with the expanse of ocean just outside the window, a pad of paper at my side and a feisty female cat named Blue on my lap. It was an exquisite moment in my life, blessed with a bounty of beauty and serenity. Giving birth to this book was effortless.

I wrote and watched the sea gulls. I walked on the beach and wrote. I wrote and listened to the waves. I drank tea and wrote.

About two-thirds of the way through the book, Dad and the spirits began laughing uproariously. Taken aback by their apparent irreverence, I asked them rather indignantly, "What's so funny?" Dad responded, "You still don't get it, do you?" I asked, "What don't I get?" He prompted me with, "What is this book all about?" "Love," I answered. "And whose house are you staying at?" Then it dawned on me: "Her last name is Love." Then from Dad, "Of course. Now you know why we waited this long to give you this book. You had to be here to receive it. It's perfect, isn't it?"

And it was.

It is with great joy that I share these poignant insights and sweet inspirations with you. Open your heart to the love that they convey. May you recognize along the way how much you are love—and are loved.

◆

*Think of these messages
as a stack of communiques from
someone who loves you very much.
You can read them randomly
if you like. You can reread your favorites.
You can place them by your bed
or in your briefcase or backpack.
You might even find that you remember
some of your preferred passages.
However you choose to partake of these
messages, do so with an open heart.
For to be open to love—to allow yourself
to be loved and loving—is to honor
yourself and the spirit that
resides within you.*

◆

LOVE

Love is the largest manifestation of God and monument to God in all of creation.

It is a manifestation because God is love—pure, unadulterated, unconditional love. Omnipotent, omnipresent love. Fulfilled, fragrant love. (Roses, after all, are God's love gift to the planet.) Content, committed love. All-embracing, effervescent love.

Love is also a monument to God. For when love links people, God is honored. When love heals and protects, God enters with force and clarity. When love binds individuals and groups, families and communities, God walks among them. When love confronts hate, when acceptance replaces rejection, when authenticity prevails over manipulation, when the light of faith overcomes the shadows of fear, God is acknowledged.

When God is loved, there can be no outcome but love.

God is love.

God is inherent in love.

God is loved wherever there is love.

To love is to be loved.

To be loved is to love.

There exists nothing but love. In the end, as in the beginning (for the two are synonymous and simultaneous) there is only love. In the end is the void, which is nothingness, which is love. In the beginning is love, which is nothingness, which is the void. In between is love, only love.

There is no other reality than love. Even in the darkest, most difficult circumstances love's flame flickers and gleams.

All things begin with love. All things end with love. All things contain the seed crystal of love, which is essence. Which is God. Which is all that is.

You are love. Your light shines, brilliant as the sun.

You are love. Your light reflects love, gentle as the moon.

You have an unlimited capacity to love. You have an unlimited capacity to be loved. Recognize that, and all else falls away. Be that, and you are at one with God.

Love, and you are God.

BOUNTY

If love is in everything and is everything, why does so much of daily life appear to be loveless? How can love be inherent in acts of darkness that defy comprehension? Such a concept seems unfathomable—if not totally unrealistic.

We acknowledge the contradiction of thinking that love is integral to apparently loveless situations. A great deal of wisdom to help you navigate the waters of darkness with courage and strength of heart has already been imparted in another book of messages in this series.* We will not address that here.

This book will focus on love—what it is, how it presents itself in your life, what lessons on love you can learn from the higher realms and how you can create and nurture more love in your life. These messages reaffirm the bounty of love—not the scarcity of it.

We recognize that love might appear to be in short supply in your life because of the superficial conditions

---

*See *A Course in Courage* in the LifeLines Library

in which you live. Below the surface love is waiting for you.

Love surrounds you. It is in the food that you eat and the water that you shower with. It is in your dreams and your thoughts (even your worried ones). Love is the venue through which the spirits who guide you communicate with you. God surrounds you with love through the evolutionary stages of your soul.

We come to you in love as we share these messages of divine wisdom with you. We walk with you in love as you read them and contemplate them. We love you in your tender clarity and your traumatic confusion.

We care beyond caring and love beyond loving.

As do you.

QUIET

Pause for a moment. What do you hear? You hear the tumult of traffic and the sweet song of birds. You hear jet engines propelling planes overhead and the wind rustling the leaves in the trees. You hear doors opening and phones ringing and the postman delivering the mail.

Pause for another moment. Listen in a different way. Now what do you hear? You hear your lungs breathing in air then releasing it. You hear your heart beating. Your body's own internal rhythms are life-giving. They are also love-inducing. For with every breath and every heartbeat, your body keeps time with the pulse of universal love.

Pause for yet another moment. Listen in an even different way. What do you hear? Silence. Nothingness. Stillness. The void. You hear all that is, which is love, which is all that you are.

Love is all that you are, whether your soul is in a living, breathing body or released from it. You are love. You always have been and always will be.

That is the wordless message whispered in the quiet.

UNCONDITIONAL

We will speak often in this book of *unconditional love.*
It behooves us to clarify what we mean by that term.

To love unconditionally is to offer the blessing of
your spirit to another without regard to what you might
achieve with that action or receive in return. Unconditional love is spirit in its most unadulterated form—the
recognition that:

♦ All of creation is united in spirit with God.
♦ You are united in spirit with God.
♦ You are united in spirit with all of creation.
♦ When you love unconditionally, you affirm this
  unity above all else.

Robust resistance to such loving emerges from many
fronts. To begin with, you arrived in this lifetime with
karmic impressions from previous sojourns on planet
earth. Many of these impressions represent your soul's
memory of experiences you had that were devoid of love
—conditional or unconditional. Even if you are consciously unaware of those memory imprints, as most people are, they still influence your perspective on what is

reasonable. Your tendency is to see unconditional love as impractical and unwarranted, if not impossible.

So because you have this predisposition, you infuse the love you feel with some measure of conditionality. For instance, you do not want to be naïve, so you decide to love someone only a little until you can determine if you might be loved in return.

You have just made your love conditional.

Or perhaps you decide to barter for your love. On some level you communicate to another, "I will give you my love if you give me the security of a checking account and a roof over my head."

Other forms of conditionality are far more dysfunctional. They take the form of a parent saying in essence to an adult son, "I will withdraw my love if you leave home and create a life apart from me."

Or a daughter may say implicitly to her parents, "I will sabotage your relationship if you don't show that you love me by letting me have my way."

Love that has any agenda other than simply being is conditional. Love that just is, whether it is acknowledged or appreciated, reciprocated or rewarded, is unconditional.

The more unconditional love you make available to others—the more you open your heart to the world—the more love will flow to you in return. It may come from surprising sources; it may arrive long after you have been loving unconditionally. In fact, it may not return to you until after this lifetime is over. But it will flow back to you many times over—powerfully and with positive goodness.

UNCONDITIONAL REVISITED

The most basic principle of all of creation is unconditional love. Why is that? It is because God loves unconditionally, and all of creation is a manifestation of the spirit of God, which is love. Everything has as its core the crystal of spirit, which is unconditional love.

To love unconditionally is to tap into that essence of all that is. To love unconditionally is also to add to the essence of all that is. To love unconditionally is to be in the spiritual flow of the God-force, giving and receiving love in equal measure.

God loves you unconditionally even if you are incapable of offering such love in return. You are loved exactly as you are by the most powerful presence in existence. You are loved without reservation, with all of your fears and foibles, doubts and duplicities.

The one steadfast truth about your life is that you are loved unconditionally. Everything else might be negotiable, but your being loved is not.

Accept that love with grace and heartfelt gratitude. It is a gift beyond imagining, abundant and constant. And it is for you. Imbibe it. Breathe it in. Fill your heart with it.

Now that your heart is full of unconditional love from spirit, what do you do with it? You can just allow it to be. It is perfectly appropriate to let yourself be loved. What a wonderful thing to do!

You could also let yourself be love.

If you can be love—if you can take some of the unconditional love that God has infused in your heart and give it away—you are loving unconditionally. If the idea of loving and wanting nothing in return makes you uncomfortable, start with a small act of unbounded love. See how it feels. Then gradually engage in even more generous acts of love.

Each time you do so, share your light as well. Let your eyes sparkle and your countenance smile. See the inner beauty in another. Acknowledge her light. Affirm that she is loved, even if you do so wordlessly.

Then try building a relationship based on unconditional love. If you want to begin with an existing relationship, recognize the areas where your love has strings attached and untie them. Ferret out your hidden agendas and toss them aside. Uncover your secret desires and let them go. Then just love the other person—exactly as he is.

If it is a new friendship, monitor your thoughts, words and actions to assure that they reflect unconditionality. The closer your relationship becomes with that person, the more likely you are to fall prey to the seductions of conditionality. It comes in thought forms such as, "I'll wait and see if..." or "When he does this, then I will..."

Loving unconditionally does not imply that you allow someone to take advantage of you. You do not need to support another in a way that enables him to avoid taking responsibility for his life. How can that be helpful to either of you? How is that aligned with spirit?

Unconditional love involves seeing him exactly as he is, accepting him without judgments exactly as he is and loving him without the expectation that he change.

That is the key—to acknowledge, accept and love without condition. The only way you can do this is to be your most authentic (and enlightened) spiritual self and to recognize his most authentic (and enlightened) spiritual self. Think of what that does for each of you. It elevates your consciousness—and that of the other—from the limitations of what you are not to the reality of what you are.

And, in reality, you are spirit in the flesh. Unconditional love is not window dressing. It is the real thing. Why not embrace it within yourself and others?

You will have to practice loving unconditionally for quite a while before you become comfortable with it. But it is one of the most potent avenues you can follow toward union with spirit. It is also a source of extraordinary meaning, mindfulness and grace.

RECIPROCITY

Perhaps you have come to believe that love must be reciprocal to make you happy. You consider the alternative—loving someone and receiving nothing in return—as a singularly unfulfilling way to relate to another.

We understand why you maintain this perspective. Unrequited love is unfortunate. It indicates that despite receiving your love, the other person is unable or unwilling to love you back—and most likely has difficulty loving at all.

But if you are wondering whether to continue loving someone who cannot or does not return that love, we have a question for you. What is the quality of your love for that individual? Is it love with attachments? Do you want to feel validated by that person? Do you hope to marry her someday? Do you want to avoid living your life alone? If so, your love is as much about you as it is about the other.

It may be love, but it is conditional. Its conditionality is rooted in what you hope to gain from the reciprocity.

When you release the need to experience reciprocity

from the love that you give, you become capable of a different kind of love. Its unconditionality enables you to love without regard for what might be returned to you. And by letting go of your expectation of reciprocity, you quite literally draw love to you.

That love may not be from the specific person you are loving, but it arrives and fills your heart nonetheless.

Reciprocity is inherent in unconditional love precisely because it is neither expected nor demanded. You withhold no love, and thus no love is withheld from you.

It is a law of the universes that the love you give without qualification returns to you at a minimum in equal measure.

So if you are feeling unfulfilled in your love—if you are angry or experiencing rejection—ask yourself what you want back from the other person. Then let go of those desires. Recognize that you cannot make someone love you back. And even if you succeeded, the love you would receive would be conditional at best and thus limited in its scope and quality.

ACCEPTANCE

If you have any intention of trying to change someone with your love—to encourage that person to overcome an addiction or adopt a new profession or lose weight—you are admitting that you do not accept that person as she is. And if you do not accept her, it means that you are judging her negatively. Wherever there is negativity because of judging, there is less opportunity to love.

Review the list you carry around with you about how you want someone you love to change. Every item on that list represents a part of you that cannot love her. The more you are able to accept her as she is right now, the more you can love her. And the more you can love her, the more ready she may become to address areas in her life that she would like to change.

She may not change. But it is more likely to happen because you have loved her without judging and thus have empowered her with your love.

Accepting another does not mean supporting a serious dysfunction or denying that it exists at all. How can that be loving behavior? Acting in a superficial way toward another to gloss over issues or problems is not love-based action.

You can and should name what needs to be named; discuss what merits discussing; explore what has depths worth exploring about the other with the other. But do so because she is ready for it, has asked for it, is open to it. And do so with total acceptance of her as she is right at this moment—not as she might be if she succeeds in making the changes you think are in her best interests to accomplish.

Love her with all of her emotional scars and superficial imperfections, then use that acceptance to build a launching pad for her potential growth and evolution. (The same holds true for yourself, you know.)

By accepting and loving without conditionality, you become a catalyst for change.

FORGIVENESS

Love and forgiveness are accomplices. They strengthen and reaffirm each other. They mirror and recall each other.

Forgiveness is inherent in unconditional love. For to love without bonds is to forgive without bounds. Some people engage in conditional forgiveness. They say, "I can forgive this and this and this. But that transgression is so egregious, so horrible, I cannot forgive it."

The decision to hold back forgiveness is the decision to hold back love. And if you decide to hold back love, you have relegated your spiritual essence to the confines of your material existence.

Forgiveness enables you to access spirit—and love— in a way that is unavailable to you otherwise. For when people challenge the depth and breadth of your love with a declaration or a deed (or an onslaught of both) requiring your forgiveness, they give you a great gift. That gift is the opportunity to experience yourself in the act of forgiveness, which is a measure of your uncompromising and unconditional commitment to loving.

You might be wondering here if forgiveness isn't actually a disservice to both the one who forgives and the forgiven. After all, if a person knows he will be forgiven no matter what, where is the incentive to take responsibility for his behavior? What is the motivation to change or improve his posture toward his own life and others'? Where does he draw the line and say, "That is truly unforgivable; therefore, I won't do it."?

We respond by saying that forgiveness is always appropriate.

All can and should be forgiven. That is the baseline. When that occurs, you infuse the circumstance with love and light instead of their opposite. That is the first step toward healing—and turnaround.

We say turnaround because forgiveness does not imply inaction or non-movement. You can forgive and encourage the other (or yourself) to address the underlying issues decisively in order not to engage in an ongoing pattern requiring forgiveness. But if the pattern continues, yes, you must continue to forgive.

Find it within yourself to forgive yourself and others. Every day. Monumental deeds and minor transgressions. Premeditated betrayals and unthinking embarrassments. Power-based affronts and ill-advised putdowns.

First, forgive. Then heal the wounds. Then address the root cause of the actions you have forgiven. But do it all with love and open-hearted acceptance. Do it all with clarity of intention and certainty of spirit.

MEMORY

Return to your soul's memory of where it has been and where it yet intends to go. For both destinations are the same.

Your soul dwells in love. It was born from love and remains there for all of eternity. It is love. It emerged from love. It returns to love. It never left love.

Your memory of love is strong and coherent. You embrace it deep within. You never completely lose sight of it, even during the most trying times.

Love is your past, present and future.

When you feel devoid of love, it is simply that you have forgotten that it is there. It has never left you. You have not grown incapable of it. You have not rejected it or become unworthy of it. You have not condemned yourself to a loveless purgatory of your own making.

No, none of these are true.

Instead, you have forgotten to notice the most fundamental aspect of your beingness.

And that is love.

Your soul's memory is both pure and blemished. On

the one hand, your soul remembers its origins and final unification with pure, absolute love. On the other hand, your soul also remembers the blemishes of the thoughts, words and deeds in which you have engaged that were less than loving.

Your soul is unbiased in its memory. It has no preferences. It records the imprint of everything you have experienced, lifetime after lifetime and during journeys in between.

How can your soul have no preferences regarding what it remembers and what it does not? Your soul's memory records the magnetic vibrations related to everything you do in and out of embodiment. It has no capacity for selective remembering or forgetting. And even if it did, there would be no basis on which to choose what to remember and what to forget.

Your soul does not judge what you think or how you feel. It simply receives these impressions and retains them with its infinite memory until you have addressed and completed your karma related to those impressions.

At that time they vanish from your soul's memory.

BACKWARD

Where love is concerned, you sometimes must go backward before you can step forward. What do we mean by that?

Often your love is associated with particular attachments—perspectives you have on what you would like the outcomes of that love to be. You do experience genuine love, but you are not as detached as you might otherwise be regarding what you want from that love.

You must take a step backward—away from those attachments—before you can love with your true capacity.

To step backward from your love is to find a place of harmony with the love exactly as it is—not as it could become. You must set aside your projections about where it might lead. You must release your ego's need to be recognized for your ability to love.

That makes your love conditional. And conditional love is compromised love.

You must harbor no desire to change anything or improve a situation or heal another's wounds with your love. For in having such agendas, you assign a purpose to your loving. And when your love has a purpose, it loses its authenticity and power.

So to step back from your love is to put some distance between you and the desires you have that are embedded in that love. Often you want so much more than love. And that wanting diminishes the essential power of the love.

If you were to understand that love is absolute unto itself—that to attach any expectations to it is to reduce its purity and thus its capacity to be infused with spirit— you would relinquish your need to link love with anything at all. For you would have faith that whatever emerges as a result of that love is wholly in spirit. It is wholly spirit. Such knowing enables you to understand that the desire for fruits from your love actually diminishes the possibility that it will yield them.

Recognize that the rewards you receive from your love are inherent in love itself—not in any ancillary effects of that love. When you can separate your desires from your love, it will offer you everything you could possibly desire. And then some.

FOCUS

When you love, where is your focus? Is it on the person or ideal or object of your love? Is it on your emotions and feelings and passions? Is it on your vulnerabilities and insecurities and unnamed worries?

Does love have a focus? Does it need one?

Love must be both focused and unfocused to be truly heartfelt. The focus of love is on the essential nature of all that is, which is love itself. To shift your focus away from that—to become preoccupied or concerned about something that appears to be other than love—is to lose your focus on the nature of love. And that creates room for something other than love.

Love must be unfocused as well. To direct your love to one person or a small number of people at the exclusion of all others is to experience only a fraction of your capacity to love. To focus your love on acquiring a possession you want is to experience very little love—if any at all.

Your love must be unfocused in that it should spring from an ability to recognize love everywhere, to see love in all and to feel love toward all. If you cannot do that (and few people can, after all) you might start by asking yourself if you believe it is true that love is inherent in all things. You may not believe that, in which case it would be impossible for you to feel love toward all. At least at first.

Love that is focused on the few and withheld from the many is the equivalent of a sun that shines one second out of every year. Yes, it is there, but only in its most abbreviated form. Love needs to be focused, but that focus is on spirit—not on the flesh or the material world.

By focusing your love on spirit, you will experience its presence in everything that surrounds you. You will find love in the wildflowers that grow amidst the rocks. You will find love in the rocks as well. You will encounter love when you pet the cat on your lap or watch the seagulls soar. You will hear love in the wind and feel it in the raindrops on your cheeks. In these moments your focus will be entirely on love, yet you will not be focusing on love in particular.

GENUINE

How can you determine if what you are feeling is love, or if it is another emotion posing as love? That is a pivotal question on your path to loving.

Most likely you have felt love often in your life. But it may not have occurred when you thought you were experiencing it. Here is what we mean.

- When your desire is more for the welfare of another than it is for your own (unless it is rooted in self-destructiveness rather than self-acknowledgement) that is love.
- When you feel deep contentment and gratitude about nothing in particular, that is love.
- When you know with crystalline clarity that your life is unfolding exactly as it should—not because good things are happening to you but because you feel that you are guided and supported and blessed —that is love.
- When you feel your heart overflowing with a benign sense of goodwill towards all that surrounds you, that is love.

+ When you want nothing more nor less, when there is nothing about your life that you would see altered for even a moment, that is love.

Of course, there are many other experiences of love. Each individual can name dozens of ways love manifests in daily life. However, you must be able to discriminate between what actually is love and what is desire posing as love.

+ If you feel or do something to accomplish a purpose or achieve a goal, you are compromising your love.

+ If you give love only when you are loved in return, you are not really giving love at all.

+ If you approach another with love so that you will be liked or respected or applauded, you are not exhibiting love.

+ If you tell yourself that you are being loving, but inside you feel flat or empty, angry or resentful, that is not love.

+ If you fear that you will lose another or be abandoned if you do not love, you will be incapable of loving.

To love as we are describing it is to accept the biggest challenge of being human. It is also to receive the most exquisite gift in return. It will serve you well to know when you are genuinely loving—and when you are not.

LIMITLESS

Your ability to love is limitless. The love that is available to you is limitless. The love inherent in all things is limitless.

How do you access such abundance?

The first step is to consider what in your life enables or encourages you to love, then commit to enhancing it. Perhaps you once volunteered to help someone less experienced or fortunate than you, and in doing so you felt a profound wave of unconditional love toward that person. Why not be there in similar ways for others? That will help you access love in abundance.

The next step is to discover when you love yourself and when you feel less than worthy.

♦ What is it about yourself that you love and respect? Strengthen those aspects of who you are. Remind yourself of their existence every day.

♦ What is it about yourself that makes you flinch? Can you imagine loving yourself anyway? Can you possibly love yourself, no matter what? We highly recommend making the attempt to do so, even if you wish you were different along a number of dimensions.

♦ Whenever you hear yourself saying, "I wish I were" stop right there and shift your thought to "I accept that I am."

You might also start improving the aspects of yourself that you can change proactively and consciously. Treat your mind, body and spirit with respect. That will enable you to tap more fully into the limitless love that surrounds you and lives within you.

Next, bring love to you with all of the little things you do daily. Pay attention to what you are thinking, saying, feeling and doing. You can shift your thoughts, emotions and actions to be more love-based. How do you do that? It is quite simple, really.

♦ When you awake in the morning, imagine yourself going through the day with love in your heart and light in your step. Then do it.

♦ When you shower, visualize that you are cleansing your energy field of negativity at the same time that you cleanse your body.

♦ When you interact with others, choose to see their light even as you realistically recognize their other aspects.

♦ When you eat, give thanks; when you walk, give thanks; when you work, give thanks; when you close your eyes to sleep, give thanks. For to be grateful for whatever your life brings to you or takes away from you is also to love God.

And to love God is to access the most limitless supply of love of all.

LAUGHTER

As long as laughter is not at the expense of another, it is a gift of love. For to see the humor in a situation is to take it less seriously. And to take it less seriously is to begin to see the love in it, even when it appears to be contrary to love.

Laughter opens the passageway to love. How can that be so? Laughter makes love a trivial matter, doesn't it? And isn't love serious business? If to love is to access God, then isn't it disrespectful to laugh in conjunction with loving?

Actually, love is not as serious as it seems. In fact, love is light—both in terms of lightness (the opposite of heaviness or weightiness) and brightness (the rays of energy that radiate from love). And what could be lighter or brighter than laughter, those hearty outbreaks that transform concern into chuckles and gloom into giggles?

Laughter is a particularly human phenomenon, although all of creation has its own way of manifesting lightness and brightness. So in a way, all of creation engages in its unique form of laughter.

Think of the meaning of the word *enjoy*—to share in joy. To laugh together is to stimulate joy. To stimulate joy is to create more room for love, for it clears out the spaces where the cobwebs of discontent have gathered and the barnacles of resentment have attached themselves.

Try this. The next time you feel yourself become weighed down by a predicament, see if instead or in addition you can identify the humor that is also there. Then laugh if you can. Who knows? At worst it will provide you with a respite from the burden you are carrying. At best it can shift or remove the burden altogether.

Either way, you have everything to gain from it, not the least of which is a greater measure of lightness of being.

ECSTASY

Love and ecstasy are synonymous in a way. In another way they are not synonymous at all. It depends on what you mean by ecstasy and what comprises the catalyst for your experiencing it.

Ecstasy that springs forth from having achieved a significant accomplishment or acquired a valuable object that you have been wanting derives from attachment. By its very nature, such ecstasy is ephemeral.

The ecstasy that erupts along with the fireworks of passion will continue as long as the passion does. But if it is not rooted in something more substantial and spiritual—namely love—it will burn itself out very quickly.

Ecstasy that enters into the space inhabited by love may be less dramatic and more subtle, less a peak experience and more a quiet glow. But it is ecstasy nonetheless.

You are not accustomed to thinking of ecstasy in such terms. You tend to believe that it must be accompanied by off-the-charts emotion.

The most profound ecstasy accompanies deep connectedness with spirit—access to the essence of God through surrender to the divine. Ecstasy becomes more a byproduct of detachment and devotion than of desire and drama. It is the ecstasy of unconditional love.

What if you could choose which form of ecstasy you have in your life? Would you rather experience the ecstasy of peaks followed by valleys or the ecstasy of a placid inner landscape? The former is more exciting and memorable; the latter is more enduring and substantial.

Perhaps you are questioning why you must choose. You want to experience both forms of ecstasy. You can. But if you are sacrificing the ecstasy of unconditional love for the ecstasy of passion or gain, you are giving up a great deal in the bargain.

Your life does not have to be boring and uneventful if you go the way of ecstatic spiritual joy. But the more you bring spirit-based ecstatic love into your life—the more you allow yourself to love and be loved unreservedly—the less you will need or even want the drama.

As you progress spiritually, you will find that you have actually increased your capability to experience ecstatic oneness with a loved one as well as with spirit. As you grow toward love-based ecstasy you will also experience greater physical and spiritual passion. Far from being opposites, the two are lively and loving bedfellows.

FALLING

You have a term to express what happens when you suddenly and completely give your heart over to another. You call it *falling in love*. That's interesting, for when you fall you lose your footing and plunge, usually without having consciously chosen to do so.

Few people decide or want to fall, whether it is from a ladder while they are painting the shutters or into love with another person. To fall is to place yourself in a situation that is out of your control until you land—on your feet or otherwise.

Falling tips the scales toward your recognition that you are not totally in charge of your life. Uncomfortable as it may seem, you benefit from being reminded of that every now and then. Much as you would like to be able to pull the strings connected to every aspect of your existence, that is just not possible. Thus, you fall.

Sometimes you fall in love. To fall in love is to be so overwhelmed by your desire to be with another or at one with another that you let go of your need to remain in control. You become vulnerable instead. This love you are experiencing is beyond your ability to calibrate. You cannot dole it out; you cannot regulate it based on the benefits you might receive compared to the costs to you.

Instead, you are wildly, madly, irrevocably in love.

Indeed, you have fallen.

The opportunity in falling is that you will experience love so overwhelming that you are forever changed by it. The risk in falling is that you may feel weakened by the experience. You no longer seem in charge of your feelings or your life. So you react by trying to gain authority over yourself again. You retreat, fence in your feelings and put boundaries around your availability. You create parameters around your love. What was born of the spirit essence—unconditional love—becomes conditional. You may have fallen, but it wasn't for long.

If you could love anther without a blueprint—if your love had no purpose other than to exist as it is—you would have no need to manage the degree to which you experience it or the amount of it that flows to another. And if you can let go of the need to regulate your love, then you are actually less likely to fall. For how can you fall if your footing is on a rock-solid foundation of love? And if you are not as likely to fall, then there is less of a probability that at some point you will want to rein in your love in order to take charge of yourself again.

For those of you who have a strong need to reassure yourselves that you have your life totally squared away, we highly recommend falling. It will give you a new perspective on how much in charge you actually are.

For those of you who have a strong desire to love without limit or recompense, we assure you that you will not fall. It simply isn't necessary.

39

FOUNDATION

The foundation of love is spirit. By the same token, love is the foundation principle of all that is.

The deeper the love, the stronger the foundation. The more unfettered the love, the more solid the foundation. The more expansive the love, the greater the impact of that foundation.

Consider the purpose of a foundation. It provides a secure base for whatever is built upon it. A well-constructed foundation can support a far more extensive and elaborate structure than a poorly engineered one. The quality of the foundation predetermines the ultimate quality of what can be created from it.

You may be wondering how love can be a foundation for anything. It is so elusive and ephemeral. It consists of high-vibration magnetic energy—not a thing or a material mass.

What kind of foundation is that?

Love is inherent in all that is. Thus it exists in anything that might create a foundation, whether it is concrete and steel or service and support. (Yes, love lives as much in concrete and steel as it does in the human heart. For everything in creation comes from spirit and returns to spirit, and therefore contains the vibration of love.)

If love is in the foundation, then love is the foundation. The greater the love, the more stable the foundation.

This is certainly true in relationships. What do you need to know more than anything else? That you are loved no matter what. That you are loved exactly as you are. That you are loved through the inevitable inconstancies and uncertainties of being human. That you are loved joyfully and endlessly.

That foundation in love is stronger than steel in bedrock. It cannot be moved; it cannot be interrupted or disrupted; it cannot erode, no matter how relentless and extreme the tests to it are.

Consider whom you currently love from such a foundation. Also consider who loves you in such a way. How does that make you feel? How do you gain strength from loving and being loved? What can you build on that love? How is it tested and retested? Where might there be cracks, and how can they be repaired? What does it affirm and how, indeed, are you blessed by it?

FEELINGS

What is the difference between love and feelings? The distinction is a significant if subtle one.

Your feelings are based on your ego's attachment to certain preferences or outcomes. For instance, you may want to be appreciated for having worked hard to contribute to a worthy cause. Your feelings are hurt when your actions are not appropriately acknowledged. Here your attachment to the rewards and recognition that derive from what you are doing is greater than your commitment to selfless service. If you are truly being of service, with nothing else in mind, it does not matter to you whether you are acknowledged for it.

Another example. Perhaps you are developing a deepening friendship with a colleague or a neighbor. You value this friendship, for it adds a measure of companionship to your life and provides you with someone to share in your life lessons. You begin to depend increasingly on this friend for counsel and guidance. At some point your friend announces that he no longer has the time and energy to play such an active role in your life. You feel wounded and rejected. What are friends for if not to be there when you need them?

Here you became attached to receiving ongoing support from another person who was unwilling to provide it. Whatever the cause, your feelings are telling you that you believe you are being denied something you want and deserve.

That is your ego talking.

Let's say, instead, that you give of yourself with nothing expected in return. You build relationships that are mutually supportive and undemanding. You care deeply and love without regard for what comes back to you as a result.

Under these circumstances, you will feel the joy and inner peace inherent in the love that is the basis of it all. Rather than focusing your attention on yourself—what you want, what you expect, what serves you the most, what is best for you, where you want things to end up— you focus on spirit. Your feelings flow in and out of undemanding spirit—not in and out of the demands made by your ego.

When you set aside your ego, with all of its insecurities, judgments and hidden agendas, you will be amazed at how much lighter and more spirited you become.

STEADFASTNESS

The human condition is punctuated by temporality and transience. People come and go; problems wax and wane; conditions change from one moment to the next.

But through it all love remains.

This steadfastness of love is what makes it such a potent quality in your life. For if love were temporal and transient, it would hold little meaning for you. It would be of little value. It would have only marginal influence, and it would certainly not be something that you would endeavor to maintain.

But despite its residence in the material world, love transcends the borders and barriers inherent in this plane. Its steadfastness redefines material reality. Love reshapes the possible, transforming limitation into limitlessness and boundaries into boundarylessness.

To be steadfast is to remain unperturbed and unaffected by the inevitable occasions that have the potential of leading love astray. To be steadfast is to refuse to compromise either the quantity or the quality of your love, however strong the weather or rough the water of your relationships. To be steadfast is to be certain of your love despite the uncertainties of another—to be caring in the face of uncaring and faithful even when your faith is one-sided.

Recall times when you have loved in a steady, steadfast way. You did not question that love; you did not reconsider whether it was a good idea to love; you refrained from using your love to cajole or coerce, manipulate or maneuver. You stood by the other and in doing so, stood by your ability to love.

Life offers you more reasons than you can possibly identify not to remain steadfast in your love. If you are looking for ways to justify your withdrawal of love, you need not wait very long or look very far.

But if you have both the commitment and the capacity for steadfastness despite all the wolves outside the door or around the corner, you will be rewarded immeasurably.

GIFT

The gift of love is the gift of spirit. And a gift of spirit is a gift of all that is. So to give love is to give everything that you have and everything that exists.

You may be thinking, "But I have so much more than love to give. I can provide financial security and a high-quality lifestyle, freedom from abuse and liberation from worries. Love is only one aspect of what I have to give."

That may be true, but in comparison to your love, all of those other gifts are a distant second in terms of their worth and meaning. For your love implies your willingness to give all that you are and all that you have. It is a gift that contains within it all other gifts.

You may be able to give everything else but love. You may be generous with your material assets, time and energy. But if you give them in a loveless way, they are hollow gifts devoid of true substance and sustenance.

If, however, you give your love and in turn offer whatever else you have, be it energy or expertise, time or tithes, your gifts will represent extraordinary spiritual abundance. For love enhances whatever it accompanies, making it far more vibrant and vital than it would be otherwise.

Ask yourself what gifts you give yourself and others. Are you more generous with others than you are with yourself, or vice versa? If so, why? What does that generosity (or lack thereof) tell you about yourself? What can you learn from your ability or inability to give fully to yourself or another? What is at the base of it all? Respect or disrespect, worthiness or unworthiness?

To withhold the gift of love is to be more human than spirit. For spirit withholds no love from anyone. God offers the gift of love throughout creation, under every circumstance.

We understand why you might hesitate to love. It does seem to open you to wounding in ways you would otherwise not be. But what is your other option? To refuse to love or refrain from loving? When you do that, you diminish the exceptional gift you have for yourself and others.

Who in your life is receiving the gift of love from you? Why do you single out that person or those people for such a potent blessing? In what ways does doing so bless you as well?

RELATIONSHIP

Love defines the relationship you have with others, be they people or plants, spirits or stars. It describes who you are in relation to them. It also suggests who you are in relation to yourself. That is the most important relationship you will have in this or any other lifetime except for the one you have with God.

Why are many relationships so problematic? For one, they seem to put you at the mercy of others' feelings toward you or their willingness to have you in their life. You might want to have an intimate relationship with a male friend, but he prefers not to get too close to you or anyone else. You recognize that and say to yourself, "Well, I cannot love him because he is incapable of loving me back."

We challenge you to reconsider this proposition. Why can't you love him anyway? Why does your love have to be dependent on his choices about love? You can still love him, even if you have no expectations of being loved in return. You can still love him, especially if you have no such expectations. That is the purest and most genuine form of love.

Suppose that eventually you do enter into a more intimate relationship with him. Things are going well for you both. You enjoy being together; you bring out the best in each other; you are mutually accepting and supportive. Before you know it, you begin to make plans for the future. You want marriage and a commitment, a new home together and a melange of other add-ons.

Your relationship, which once was uncluttered with expectations, becomes overburdened with them. Rather than living in the moment—appreciating your relationship exactly as it is right now and allowing it to unfold in the future—you project a staggering collection of hopes and dreams onto it.

We do not mean to imply that you should not contemplate marriage and commitment, having a family and growing old together. Rather, we urge you to make room for those potentialities to present themselves in their own time—to emerge as an outgrowth of your unconditional love instead of an extrapolation from one step in the here and now to ten thousand steps further down the road.

Human existence revolves around relating and relationships. Much of your karma is relationship-based. You will complete and heal your karma in relationship with others. The choice to love one another without expectation or attachment will enable you to make extraordinary karmic progress. It will also bring a great deal of light into dark places everywhere.

The choice to pile attachments onto your love like toppings on an ice cream sundae may taste delicious, but only momentarily. Quickly it will become too much for you and the other. What you once anticipated you now regret; what you once had high hopes for is now extinguished; what you once saw as a catalyst for rebirth feels lifeless.

Enter into relationships of all sorts. But when you do, be aware of the paraphernalia you also bring to them. The more of it you can leave behind, the more likely the relationship will be mutually beneficial, growth-enhancing and, most of all, loving.

LOSS

Loving can make you feel susceptible to loss. For eventually the object of your love may leave your life, through death, distance or the deterioration of your relationship. That loss hurts all the more if your love is deep and all-encompassing.

You cannot protect yourself from loss. There are no alarm systems to keep it from occurring or insurance policies to make amends after the fact. The loss of a loved one—maybe many loved ones—will occur in your lifetime. That is a probability more than a potentiality, unless you die at a very young age.

What can you do to prepare yourself for such losses?

You may initially consider a protection mechanism that many people employ even if they are unaware of it. It involves limiting your exposure to loss by giving your love only to a few and only when it is a sure thing. You love if there is a strong likelihood that you will be loved in return and that the person will not leave your life unexpectedly through death or a decision to depart.

That strategy leads to a singularly unfulfilling and

meaningless life. But if the price of loving—being exposed to loss—seems too high to you, you are likely to opt for lovelessness.

Another option is to move in and out of love every chance you get. Then you can say that even if you face subsequent loss, the love was worth it. This is the "just do it" approach to loving, which throws caution to the wind and vulnerability out the window. Your attitude is, relish the love in the moment and don't think about the consequences.

A final alternative is to love to the depths of your soul, without calculation or desperation or self-protection. You love with the understanding that unto itself your ability to love is enough. You love knowing that there might be loss, but that love lives on just as spirit lives on. You love with the belief that love creates strength instead of vulnerability and fullness instead of emptiness.

You love for the sake of loving, and nothing else.

When you love in this way, you transcend loss—even when someone you hold most dear leaves you; even when you cannot imagine life without a loved one; even when you lose someone who is your best friend and closest companion and most cherished counselor all rolled into one.

Yes, you will grieve the loss. But you will also celebrate the love as it existed and will continue to exist throughout lifetimes—and especially throughout this one in particular.

PRECIOUS

Love is the most precious aspect of all of creation because it is the essence of God. But unlike objects that are considered precious because they are scarce, love is available in unlimited supply.

If you can access as much love as you want, then why is it so precious? Doesn't its pervasiveness make it less precious, less valuable?

It depends on whether you take a supply-and-demand approach, believing that greater demand and restricted supply make something more precious, or a love-and-light approach.

Let's look at the latter. Suppose that you start with a base of love toward your son. That love is precious to begin with. Over the years you strive to understand and accept him. The two of you spend time together exploring new ideas and talking on the phone, trusting each other increasingly. Your love grows more vital as a result, and thus even more precious. You find that you can disagree and transcend your differences without residual negativity and judgments. That adds to the precious nature of your relationship. You build one of the most valuable relationships in your life—one that grows into mutual unconditional love.

And that is most precious of all.

Let's consider, at the other end of the continuum, the supply-and-demand approach to precious love. Here your intention would be to increase the demand or desire for your love on the part of your son while you decrease the supply of it that you make available to him. The more he wants and the less you provide, the more precious it becomes. Or so it would seem.

We have already shown you how the opposite is, in fact, the case. When you come to realize that giving your love freely creates more love for you to receive, you will let go of the need to limit artificially the love you make available to another. When you release the need to see love as a self-serving transaction and instead see it as an integral aspect of the pulse of life, you will see the spirit that resides in it.

And that spirit is most precious.

COMMITMENT

Commitment is both a problematic and a promising component of many love-based relationships.

Commitment is generally perceived as an aspect that strengthens love, for it portends longevity, exclusivity and intentionality. People assume that a committed love has a better chance of weathering the storms and droughts than an uncommitted one.

To some extent that is the case. And yet we see example after example of supposedly committed love that is in fact short-lived; of committed love that does not survive even minor altercations; of committed love that represents nothing more than a momentary interest that lasts until someone better or more interesting comes along.

What is commitment, anyway, and how does it manifest in a genuine way?

Commitment is love-based, not negotiation-based. It derives from unfettered love. Rather than creating shackles, as many people perceive commitment to do, it unshackles those unified in love.

Commitment reaffirms love-based union. Its message

is this: "I love you now, and I will love you always—whatever the configuration of our relationship, whether we are together or apart. I will hold you dear and support you in your personal growth and spiritual evolution. I will treat you with respect and give you my most authentic self. I will be there to help you through your distress and to celebrate your successes. I will share common ground with you. I will also respect our differences and preserve our individuality."

That is true commitment.

Commitment is less about the quantity of your togetherness (how long you are together, how often and how unilaterally) and more about the quality of your togetherness (how you share and care, give and receive). To commit is to offer your love, your spirit and your essential self to another. That is the most fundamental—and inviolable—commitment of all.

MARRIAGE

One tradition pervades most of the cultures on planet earth, and that is the institution of marriage. Its highest purpose is to unite two people beyond the physical—to enable them to come together in a spiritual union that forms the basis of their relationship together and that of the family they may create.

For a time marriage deteriorated into an arrangement authorized by the religious order to unite political forces and power bases. It became less about the relationship between husband and wife, and more about merging bloodlines to create a more impenetrable political presence or financial empire. Those marriages were often in name only. The union of husband and wife on the spiritual planes was rare because they did not love each other initially and never grew to love each other later.

Such marriages still occur today, although they are less frequent. In addition, women have gained far more personal and societal power than they had before. In many cultures women now have the latitude to decide on their own if, when and whom they will marry and how they will contribute to that marriage.

Assuming that this is the case, what does marriage represent? What opportunities does it present? What does it offer beyond the legal endorsement of the state and the religious approval of the church?

The commitment to marry another occurs when two people share a love that is so deep and meaningful, they decide that they want to build a life and perhaps a family together around that love.

But the marriage commitment goes beyond that. It focuses on the union of two people spiritually—the union of two souls as one before God and their friends and family. This union is a call to spirit—to bring spirit into the couple's daily life.

Of course, there are other aspects to the commitment as well—not the least of which is the legal joining of two people. But central to marriage is spirit, which is love.

Marriage provides the couple an opportunity to join in love and grow together in love, learning, becoming and exploring more than they could have done alone. It offers each one a chance to experience the poignant power of unconditional love, perhaps for the first time. It protects the fragility of a relationship with the potency of commitment—the mutual decision to traverse the inevitable detours and difficulties together, without splitting apart.

Love-based marriage is a great blessing to all of creation, for it pulsates with an ongoing magnetic energy of the highest vibration. This contributes to the overall healing of individual and planetary negativity. It helps propel souls and societies toward dynamic spiritual evolution. For that we are most grateful.

But more importantly, love-based marriage opens the door for people to pursue their own spiritual journey with greater vitality—and with the support of another. The path to spirit is open to all. Some choose to walk it relatively alone. Others find that having a partner to walk with them makes the pilgrimage even more loving and spirited.

If you choose to travel alone, we wish you love.

If you choose to travel with a partner, we wish you love.

SEXUALITY

To offer messages about love and not address the sexual aspect of love would be like describing a regional cuisine and leaving out the spices. For sexuality does add spice to your life—and to a relationship. It also contributes energy and excitement to a loving relationship.

But sexuality is far more than that. Yes, it does enable the procreation of the species—not an unimportant benefit. But that, too, is less significant than the spiritual and love-expanding aspects of sexual union.

The opportunity in any loving relationship is that the partners will form a union that transcends the limitations of the third dimension and transports them to the higher realms of union with all of creation. As you can imagine, one's consciousness must soar far outside of the body to access spirit in such a way.

One of the most effective ways to stimulate such union with spirit is through the act of lovemaking. It is one of life's great paradoxes that what starts as a purely physical act between two people can culminate in a way that takes them so far out of their bodies.

Whatever honors the love-based union of two people, whether it is their sexuality or their mutual responsibility for each other, honors the spirit that lives in both. And whatever honors that spirit stimulates access to and union with God.

Sexuality enables union on many levels to occur: the union of two people physically; the union of their souls in spiritual oneness; and the union of that oneness with the One. Far from being simply an act of seduction (although that is totally appropriate to stimulate the physical aspects of the union) lovemaking is indeed an act of making or creating love. And that love links the partners more closely with each other and with the divine.

Be aware of these levels of union that can occur with your lovemaking. Relish the physical union, for unto itself it reaffirms your togetherness. Be grateful for the spiritual union you experience through your sexuality, for it honors the larger reality of your relationship. Give thanks for the oneness with spirit that you encounter together, for in that resides the purity of your love.

PARTNERSHIP

In love there is ample space for partnership—the mutual responsibility that is shared by two people. Partnership is fueled by love and, in turn, it strengthens that love. For it enables both people to experience the comfort of being able to trust and depend on each other.

The most basic component of a partnership is mutuality—the commitment of both people to contribute their time and energy, creativity and expertise for the larger benefit of both. Their mutuality arises from the ability of the partners to trust and respect each other enough to be mutually vulnerable. Without this foundation a workable partnership is impossible.

Love enables you and another to take a leap of faith with each other and begin living in partnership rather than self-sufficiently alone. We use the term *leap of faith* advisedly, for at first that is exactly what it is. Until you have some experience that the partnership will actually manifest mutuality, you must act on your belief that it will, then take steps together toward that end.

In a partnership a relative balance of contribution

and benefit, commitment and gain is necessary. Of course, the dynamic will vary over the short term depending on each person's ability to contribute to the partnership and each person's requirements from the partnership. But over the longer term this balance must be preserved. Without it there is no partnership. Without it what may have begun as a partnership devolves instead into a one-sided way of relating.

You may be wondering how mutuality and unconditional love can coexist. After all, mutuality implies that the partners pay attention to what they are giving and receiving. And to be unconditional is to let go of the need to receive anything in return for what you are giving.

These two approaches are not at odds. Two people can love each other unconditionally and be in a healthy, dynamic partnership. They can give generously from the heart and work consciously together to assure that their commitment and responsibilities, benefits and rewards are relatively balanced.

Yes, you do love each other and you live together in the real world. Your partnership helps you both approach life more wisely—and lovingly.

COMPANIONSHIP

A lover can also be a companion. And some of the best companions are also lovers.

Companionship is a central aspect of a loving relationship. There is contentment in companionship, coupled with a blessed awareness that you are not required to be responsible for accomplishing everything yourself.

A companion can share in your joys and celebrate your successes. A companion can also ease the pain of failure and help you recover from loss. A companion can prepare dinner and take out the garbage, clean the gutters and walk the dog (not inconsequential benefits!).

The key to healthy companionship is to maintain your separateness in the context of your togetherness. Too much togetherness can overpower and overburden a relationship between companions, causing them to feel more suffocated than supported.

How do two people remain separate and together? Consider the best of what companionship has to offer. It allows you to choose to do some things with another, whether it makes the doing easier or more expedient or more enjoyable. It also allows you to choose not to do everything together.

Too much companionship causes the companions to lose touch with who they are individually. Too much apartness causes the individuals to lose sight of the boons and blessings of their companionship. But independence and togetherness form a lovely combination that enhances the facets of both.

Companionship is not so much about passion and drama as it is about comfortableness and contentment. A companion is just as happy seeing you in your favorite old shirt and jeans as in your fanciest wardrobe. A companion knows how to be with you when you are concerned and when you are carefree. A companion helps you see the bright side of things when that is what you need and, equally importantly, is there when that is the last thing you need. A companion brings you flowers when you are sick and chocolates when you are well and hugs in between for no particular reason.

Recognize the unassuming gifts embedded in the panorama of companionship. Collectively they form a tapestry of love, woven a thread at a time.

SINGLE

With all of this talk of marriage, partnership and companionship, you may be wondering if we are implying that the life of someone who is single and living alone is less loving or fulfilling. We have no such intention. In fact, whether you are single or married is irrelevant to your ability to love. It also bears no relationship to the love you have in your life and the measure of spirit you are bringing into your life.

The life of a single person is uniquely fulfilling in that you have the opportunity to explore the depths of your spiritual existence through your aloneness. Of course, you have many relationships with friends and family, work colleagues and neighbors. In fact, you may spend less time in solitude than others who are living under the same roof with someone else.

Nonetheless, you do have a significant chance to create time to be alone if that is a priority for you. We encourage you to do just that. Time alone enables you to blanket your life with the peace and serenity that derives from stillness and solitude. That is a blessing.

But what does solitude have to do with love? Isn't loving all about how you feel towards another individual? Doesn't it take two (at least) to love?

If you are talking about relationship-based love, then of course that is the case. But there are many other forms of love that do not require a recipient of your love.

Think of your solitude as time with spirit—your own spirit and the guides who accompany you throughout the day. At these times you can access the wisdom that is available to you, in all of its profundity and practicality. You can be reaffirmed and reassured, energized and endowed with light. In other words, you can love and be loved.

Such occasions can occur when you are walking, sitting quietly or listening to music. Spirit cherishes these moments, for you become a much more open channel to receive their gifts and messages at such times.

Those who are single also have many opportunities to learn how to ask for assistance from others. After significant time living alone, people typically fall into two patterns: the "I am perfectly capable of doing this myself, thank you" group and the "I am helpless. Can you do this for me?" group. Both extremes are just that—extreme.

A more appropriate and spiritually balanced option is to clarify your own capabilities and needs. Then assess whether they fall too far on one side of the self-sufficiency continuum or the other. If you find it difficult to ask others for assistance, you probably have an issue with receiving. What is at the root of it? How can you begin to release its hold on you?

If you choose to do little for yourself, instead asking regularly for favors from others, identify why you cannot be more self-reliant. Are you feeling insecure or selfish? Have you found that it is easier to get others to do things for you than to accomplish them yourself? How can you take steps to become more self-sufficient?

To be single is, by design or default, to live your personal life more alone than you would with a partner or family. It comes with many responsibilities and rewards, not the least of which is learning to give and receive in the best possible way. When you do that, you exhibit utmost respect for yourself as an independent person and for your friends and family who are there for you.

FOREVER

Love and *forever* are two words that are used together more often than you might think. People declare, "I will love you forever," meaning, usually, that they love the other so much now, they cannot imagine that love will not exist from here on out. Traditional marriage vows include the phrase "till death do us part" as substitute language for "forever."

Love is a "forever" kind of word, but not in the way it is frequently used. Love does exist forever. In the beginning was love; in the end is love. In between is love. Love is forever because it is synonymous with spirit. God is love, and that love is forever. It is immortal.

But is mortal love really forever? Can it be?

Yes, mortal love can be forever. That is the dance of karma. You can love another soul as it takes multiple embodiments concurrent with yours and in between embodiments. That love can span millennia of earth-years and far longer than that in the higher dimensions. Love can be forever in that way.

This perspective reframes the meaning of "till death

do us part." Actually, death does not separate you from a loved one in any way besides the physical. Death does not part two souls who love each other deeply. That love simply must traverse longer distances and multiple dimensions to be shared. It remains vital when one soul is still in a physical body and the other is no longer, and when both have left their bodies after death to unite in the higher planes.

Mortal love is forever in another way as well. When you love someone, you access spirit with that love. You affirm the existence of a force greater than yourself and your relationship, greater than all the love in all the relationships and friendships and families on the planet. The love you access is so immense, it makes all else pale in comparison. When you love another you find the pathway to God's love. You are God's love. And that love is forever because God is forever.

So when you tell someone that you will love him or her forever, think of all of the depths of meaning embedded in that declaration. Neither say it glibly nor take it lightly.

True love is forever. It is a blessing and a responsibility, for to love is to transcend the smallness of judging, controlling and manipulating.

To love forever is to be love toward another, and to allow the other to be.

That is love.

That is forever.

HEALING

Love heals. Love is balm for the wounded soul, surcease from sorrow, release from pain.

How can we declare that love heals when so many people who are dearly loved face physical and mental disabilities? Where is there an indication that they are healed in any way whatsoever? How does love have any healing influence over them at all?

You have evidence in the history of the planet of the power of love to heal. Your spiritual prophets were and are healers; shamans were and are healers. Even members of the medical profession are finding a strong connection between prayer and healing.

All of these venues for healing function on the basis of love, which is spirit. Spirit can heal even the most deadly disease by shifting the magnetics at which the diseased aspect of the body vibrates. The catalyst is love. When love in its purest form enters the body, afflicted cells can no longer remain in a state of disease.

So yes, love can and does heal in the literal sense of the word.

But how about more symbolic forms of healing? Perhaps someone is profoundly hurt after having loved another and then been betrayed or rejected. The wounds cut deeply; the resulting scars of self-protection are considerable. The person is not about to open himself to more pain by loving another again so completely.

What is the one force that will heal those wounds and relax his defenses? It is love. If he experiences unconditional love from others—people who genuinely hold his welfare above all else—he might eventually begin to trust in love again.

There exists no effect more powerful than love. When love enters into a situation, be it physical or metaphysical, it dissipates all other forces at work. You may not always see evidence of this through spontaneous healing or psychological realignment, but the impact of that love has registered at a deep level regardless.

When someone in your life needs to be healed, love that person in every way possible. Bring spirit into his life with music and meditation, flowers and fragrance, candles and color. Do so with one intention: that God's will be done. Create a healing environment, energize it with your love, then surrender the outcome to God.

Do the same for yourself if healing is something you need or desire. Loving yourself is never inappropriate. And who knows? The healing effects of your love may strengthen far more than your body.

UNIVERSALITY

You may be thinking, "I love some people, but I do not see spirit in all things. I may see spirit in those I love, but that is different because I love them. I don't necessarily love all things."

That is an honest assessment of how many people approach love—finding joy in togetherness with the object of their affection, but not in a generalized way beyond that. We applaud your forthrightness about how you feel—your understanding of what you are capable of experiencing and what seems beyond your grasp.

That is a good place to begin.

But that is all it is—a good place to begin. If you have been blessed with the ability to love and have been introduced to people in your life to whom you can give that love, why stop there? What is keeping you from seeing God in others as well?

- ◆ Is it because you do not know them well enough? If so, can't you love them anyway?
- ◆ Is it because they have done something you do not approve of? If so, can't you forgive them?

◆ Is it because you think you have only so much to
  give, and you would rather share it with the people
  closest to you who you believe deserve it the most?

What if you understood that you have an infinite
supply of love—that you couldn't possibly run out of
love, even if you loved all of creation? (And that is a lot
of love.)

What if you realized that every shred of love that you
give to others comes back to you? It is returned by others
who love you; it is returned in the form of karmic healing
and completion; it is returned by the spirits who guide
you and help you in mission and lesson; it is returned by
God, who loves you dearly and unconditionally.

You live within the flow of universal love. It surrounds you when you love universally and when you do
not. The more universal your love, the greater your ability to imbibe that love.

JOY

The joy of love freely given is unsurpassed for both the giver and the recipient. Embedded in love is a home for spirit. When spirit is present, joy prevails.

The more you experience love, the more aware you become that a certain lightness has entered your life. Problems no longer seem quite so insurmountable; people don't appear to be quite so irredeemable; traumas are not quite so devastating. You carry within you a sense that you can get through just about anything, although you would really rather not have to prove it again and again.

That is the work of love.

Love and lightness float on the same impulse. They surround situations with the essence of manageability (at a minimum) and merriment (quite often). Have you ever been moved to joy by a circumstance that would appear to others to be singularly lacking in it? The lightheartedness you feel is in keeping with the spirit you see residing in what is occurring.

To love completely is to find joy in all things and see

spirit in all things. Your heart sings in joy and your spirit soars with ecstatic wonderment.

Eruptions of joy occur because you recognize that you are so blessed by spirit—that the love you feel is so extraordinary, and yet so present in your most ordinary life—that you experience bliss. You see the world through love-inspired lenses, and those lenses enable you to anticipate the celebration of life all around you.

You have been gifted with moments such as these. They may have been fleeting, but you still experienced them. Many more are available to you. All you need to do is open yourself to the possibility that joy and love are yours, always and eternally.

Love invades your life with a festival of gossamer light and vivid color. It mitigates the shades of gray that surround you, piquing your senses. No greater joy exists than that which flows from a feast of love, whatever form it takes. We watch your aura gleam and glow as you love and enjoy life.

Love is as much a gift to God as a gift from God. Offer it—and receive it—with the jubilant spirit in which it is intended.

FAMILY

You are a member of many families, only one of which consists of those to whom you are related by blood.

To begin with, you are in God's family—the most magnificent collection of spirits imaginable. God is your spiritual father and mother, the catalyst for your creation; the source of your birth, rebirth and eternal life; the organizing principle around which all of creation revolves.

You are God's love child.

As a member of God's family you carry in your genetic code the seed of spirit. It is what gives you life; it is what provides you with wisdom and insight; it is what helps you see far beyond your current reality and into a more profound one than you ever imagined possible.

That is your inheritance from God.

Then you are in the family of humankind—a particular species of life that has been arriving on planet earth for tens of thousands of years. As a member of this family you carry God-consciousness within. You also carry the collective consciousness of all of humanity in your cellular memory.

You are born. You live life as best you can (and hopefully even better). You die and return home to the higher dimensions, then you are born again. This is the pattern that most people in the family of man and woman follow. You share this common heritage. It is different from the heritage of other souls throughout creation because it is being played out on planet earth.

You are also a member of your birth family, the genetic heritage of which was passed down to you by your biological mother and father. This birth family may or may not be the one that surrounded you as you were growing up or that constitutes your family now. But it is relevant in that you carry hereditary genetic encoding. This encoding plays a significant role in your health, intelligence, psychology, strength and, of course, your physical appearance. Whatever your biological family gave you at birth predetermines many physiological and psychological aspects of your life.

And finally, there is the collection of blood relatives and friends who, based on their central role in your life, constitute your extended family. Most of the key people in this group have been with you in prior lifetimes, pursuing the journey with you and discovering with you common milestones and memories. This is the family with whom you share the most pivotal aspects of this lifetime, and who most likely accompany you between lifetimes in the higher realms.

You share a great deal of history, planetary and otherwise. Even if you do not consciously recall your extensive prior experiences together, you have the context of this lifetime in which to frame your mutual support and karmic growth.

Love is the aspect that connects all of your families. It is the common denominator of all of life. It also forms the common denominator of your familial affiliations. Whatever family you focus on, be it God's or the one you have with your parents and siblings, children and relatives, you know that love is present.

CREATION

Love is a phenomenally creative force. It unleashes the creative potential that serves as a catalyst for all sorts of things, from innovation to insight and offspring to original art.

The act of creating is an act of love, so aligned with spirit is it.

Love stimulates creativity by enabling you to tap into something larger than yourself. The unbounding of creative potential is a natural outgrowth of that.

When you are acutely aware of the patterns that affect nature—that enable the flowers to bloom and grass to grow and fish to swim in the sea—you can create with greater sensitivity toward the natural order of things. And when you create with such sensitivity, you tap into the spirit seed of all of creation, which is God's love. When God's love lights the way for your creations, they will be remarkable indeed.

Many people attempt to be creative in a vacuum. They believe that inspiration is a function of thinking and that creativity derives from systematic research and development. Nothing could be further from the truth. To inspire means, quite literally, to infuse with spirit. To create is to produce something that did not exist before, at least in its current form. And to produce something new requires spirit.

We do not discount the importance of intelligence and expertise, hard work and methodical investigation in the process of preparing to create. But they represent only a fraction of what actually contributes to the creative process.

The rest is spirit.

Recall something you created recently. Was the end result more a function of step-by-step plodding or out-of-the-blue leaps forward? If it was more the latter, you can count on the fact that spirit was at work. The more surprising the results, the greater extent to which spirit informed the process. The more effortless your role, the more you were guided by spirit.

Allow love to fuel the creative force in your life. The expansiveness of love shifts your perspective from the reasons you cannot create something to the reasons you can.

SENSUALITY

Erotic love is as natural as the fragrances and flavors that grow from the soil in a well-tended garden. Yes, you grow fruits and vegetables to sustain your body. But you also plant particular ones because they taste good to you. They stimulate your senses. The same is true for flowers and grasses, trees and shrubs, which you select for their visual beauty and delicate fragrance.

Sensuality in a loving relationship enables the partners to express through a touch, a word, a movement or even a look what they perhaps cannot find the language to convey. There are many ways in which people communicate, and one is through the senses. There are just as many ways in which partners enable each other to partake of the love they share, and one is through the senses.

God would not have created such a gorgeous, sensual environment as planet earth if it were not meant to stimulate your senses. What is more sensual than a riot of color at sunset or the flicker of flames and the scent of burning wood in a fireplace? What could be more delicious than a meal prepared with fresh ingredients and herbs? What is more comforting than a hug, more expressive than a touch, more generous than the act of love?

When you take time to consider the profusion of sensual stimuli available to you on a daily basis, it is a wonder people choose to do anything but indulge in it all.

Loving another motivates people to take special care in creating pleasures that are gifts to the senses. A father may make his daughter's favorite dinner to acknowledge her achievement. A family might spend a week's vacation at the beach so that everyone can enjoy the surf and the sand between their toes. A lover may don silk for the way it flows and feels against the skin. A woman may purchase a watercolor painting because looking at it transports her to a place of deep serenity.

Overindulging in sensuous pleasures to the point of obsession can become abusive and hedonistic, but an appropriate measure of sensuality is a delightful way to live in love—and spread the unique joy of being human.

PULSE

All of creation pulses with the vibration of love. Every rock on every planet in every galaxy throughout the universes is in attunement with the love vibration. The light emanating from all of the souls in existence everywhere pulses with the love vibration.

Everything in existence shares one common element. And that is love, which is spirit, which is God.

Differentness is created by the varying degrees to which the love vibration influences each body of matter, and the energetic pulse at which it vibrates. The denser the matter, the slower the vibration. The more light-filled the entity, the higher the vibration.

Although vibratory capacities vary enormously, their infusion with the love of spirit does not vary. God's love pulses in everything that is, in equal measure. God does not favor the tree over the sea or the diamond over the chalk.

Given that, you may conclude that the pulse of love maintains some sort of homeostasis and can be neither enhanced nor negated by your influence. But that is not the case. Just as God is in all things, all things are inter-connected in spirit.

The more capacity you have to love, the more you strengthen the love vibration innate in all things. The more you meld spirit into your being, the higher the vibration at which your soul pulses.

When you love unconditionally, you are accessing spirit that pulses at a higher frequency. This acts as a tuning fork of sorts, enabling the spirit vibrating in all matter around you to raise its own vibration to become more in tune with yours.

For instance, you may enter a friend's home and sense, "This is a happy house." What you are feeling is not just her own happiness, but the degree to which the house itself and everything in and around it are vibrating in time with her contentment.

Everything pulses to the rhythms of spirit. Every-thing has the capacity to alter those rhythms based on the love field in which it resides.

So to be more loving is not just to take a step closer to God yourself. It also enables you to help other aspects of creation to pulse with the vibration of love, and in their own way move closer to God.

DESIRES

When you consider what you desire, imagine that the one most precious thing anyone could have or acquire is available to you in abundance. And if that most desirable commodity is there for the taking in an unlimited supply, then what else could you desire more?

Perhaps you have some desires that are not or have not been met. You want a stronger body, more authentic relationships, more fulfilling work, more time to relax and renew. You have taken steps to achieve each of these objectives, but they continue to elude you.

This frustrates and saddens you, leading you to become even more entangled in your feelings of being deprived.

What if you could set aside those desires, even temporarily, and replace them with a different notion? What if you understood that you already have what you desire, which at its core is to be loved? What if you understood that you have already accomplished what you want, which is to love? How would you feel if you recognized that you can have and be exactly what you want, and that all of the desires that remain beyond your grasp are just minor, irritating distractions?

Even though they may be distractions, they matter to you. How can it be irrelevant to want to derive more meaning from your work or to desire to be in a loving relationship with a partner? Those desires are in keeping with spirit, aren't they?

Indeed, they are. But you must recognize that the path to achieving them is to let go of your desire for them and focus instead on bringing love into all that you are and all that you do, every moment of every day. If you imbue everything with love, how can you not have a loving life? And if your life is loving, what else could you desire? What could you possibly be lacking?

Desire causes you to pay inordinate attention to what you do not have at the expense of appreciating what you do have. Often they are identical—opposite sides of the same coin. You already have everything that you desire; you just do not recognize that yet.

Why not turn your assumptions upside down? Why not grant that you are loved beyond your deepest desires? Why not realize that you love beyond your deepest longings?

It is true, you know.

It is also time that you begin to believe it.

LIVING LOVE

If you experience serenity throughout the day, even if you are busy accomplishing many responsibilities, you are living in love.

If you are at peace, no matter what the external conditions may be, you are living in love.

If you feel joy, which manifests not so much as ecstatic highs but as a deep inner sense of being blessed and the gratitude that accompanies such a realization, you are living in love.

If you are frequently thankful for an abundance of gifts from spirit, no matter what your material or physical abundance represents, you are living in love.

If you have the sense that you are guided and supported—that the invisible hand of spirit is pointing the way for you to choose appropriately, grow exponentially and deepen your inner knowing—you are living in love.

If at the end of the day you feel that whatever is, is right and good—that your life is unfolding exactly as it should—you are living in love.

There will be times, of course, when you do not feel

gratitude or when peacefulness eludes you. There will be times when try as you might, you cannot stem the tide of concern or worry. You are human, after all, and you are likely to notice on occasion (or more frequently than that) that you are incapable of dredging up any love at all.

Of course, you cannot force yourself to feel love that is not there, and you should not pretend that you love when you do not. But you can find within yourself a modicum of love toward someone or something. Locate it, then dwell on that. Make it bigger than it was. Make it huge. Make it your preoccupation if you have to.

It is better to maintain a one-pointed focus on a tiny glimmer of love, even if that glimmer seems irrelevant or inconsequential, than to expend your time and energy reminding yourself of how awful everything is. Where does that get you but feeling even worse?

Everyone has the capability to live in love, for everyone feels a measure of love toward someone or something. And when you choose to live in love (for love does not appear out of nowhere by happenstance; you actively choose to love or not to love) you will find that the love in and around you expands. It shines within a larger context and community around you, enabling everyone to live in more and more love.

Reaffirm the serenity and gratitude that prevail when love is present.

Bring love into your life by bringing your love to life.

DISSOLVE

In the beginning, before creation, there was nothing but love. In the end, after all that exists has dissolved into love, there will be nothing but love. In between there is nothing but love, for the beginning and the end occur simultaneously.

Therefore, there is nothing but love. Anywhere. At any time. In all of God's universes.

All is love.

We recognize that this is an enigmatic concept for you to incorporate into your consciousness. Nonetheless, we ask you to begin to move your thinking in that direction.

If all is love, then you are nothing but love. You have the potential of embodying love and nothing else.

As you progress spiritually, you will find that the biggest change you encounter is that you are more loving. You feel love for friends and strangers alike. You love the birds chirping and the cats purring, breezes blowing and snowflakes falling. To you the planet is awesomely beautiful and the heavens inspire you beyond imagining.

Your judgments, attachments and preferences dissolve into love. Many of the hardships that sidetracked you before become irrelevant. You are content with whatever the moment brings, for each moment is perfect. Each moment is an expression of love.

When you move closer and closer to karmic completion—when it no longer becomes necessary to return for another embodiment because you have replaced all of your previous life patterns with love—your soul dissolves the human aspects of your individuality and enters into oneness with spirit.

Imagine a time when this occurs throughout planet earth, when there is nothing but love. Nothing. At that point the vibration of all that is on the planet will shift, becoming one with spirit. The planet itself will dissolve into essence.

The love vibration that pulses in everything will become the sole element in everything, replacing matter and mass with love. The planet will be nothing but love and light and magnetic vibration.

And all that is currently in this dimension will be one with the One.

LETTERS

These messages are love letters from spirit to you. We have found many ways to say the same thing to you again and again.

You are loved.

It is irrelevant whether you feel worthy of such love; whether you can accept unconditional love; whether you believe that love is really there through your darkest hours.

You are loved.

We want you to know that. What you do with this information is up to you, although we are optimistic that it will be a source of solace and sustenance, strength and stability for you.

Think of these messages as a stack of communiques from someone who loves you very much. You can read them randomly if you like. You can reread your favorites. You can place them by your bed or in your briefcase or backpack. You might even find that you remember some of your preferred passages.

However you choose to partake of these messages, do

so with an open heart. For to be open to love—to allow yourself to be loved and loving—is to honor yourself and the spirit that resides within you.

You can, of course, send us communiques as well. They might take the form of journal entries, prayers or conversations with loved ones. They can be acts of generosity and kindness toward others, words of love to another or unselfish caring and giving.

All of these are love letters to God. Every time you speak or act from a place of love, you are returning God's love. You are answering the love letters you have received from the beginning of your soul's existence.

If you gain nothing else from this collection of messages, let it be that you understand and accept a little more than you did before that your life already is love— that love is not being withheld from you.

And in understanding that, perhaps you can come to recognize your own capacity to love. For it is as immense as the sky; it is as brilliant as the stars on a clear night; it is as beautiful as the rays of sunshine glistening down through the trees.

You are all of that and more. For you are spirit.

You are love.

REJOICE

We rejoice in the fact that you have received our love letters to you and have begun to experience the power of the love we feel toward you. You bless us with your spirited outlook on life and your commitment to your spiritual evolution.

You are progressing because you are allowing love into your life. You are progressing because you are more loving throughout your life. We see the extent to which you are imbibing and integrating love. This overwhelms us with joy and gratitude.

We also rejoice because you have given us the opportunity to be heard. For to communicate messages of love and then know that they are understood and taken to heart is to be effectively in service to the One.

We link arms with you in spirit, forming a circle of divine love that cannot and will not be broken. We care for you in the most loving way. We are pilgrims and partners together on the path to the One.

So we close this collection of messages with the reassurance that your progress on your journey to spirit will be guided by love and fueled by love, decorated with love and inspired by love. There is no more loving presence than you, for you are God incarnate.

May you walk in joy. May you live in love. May you go in peace.

May you rejoice in the wonder of your ability to love and be loved, always and always.

Gates McKibbin never imagined that after spending twenty years as a corporate executive, management consultant and adjunct college professor specializing in strategic and organizational renewal, she would publish messages channeled from her deceased father, John McKibbin. For most of her adult life she had balanced a fulfilling professional career and a fascinating spiritual quest. Then quite unexpectedly her father, who visited the earth plane frequently after his death, began sending telepathic messages for her to write in her journal.

Three years and six books later, Gates has now added "Inspirational author and speaker" to her resume. She still helps business executives navigate turbulent change, and she also seeds the planet with insights from the spirit world. To complement the LifeLines Library, Gates has developed a collection of thematic LifeLines note pads featuring her favorite one-liners from the books.

Born and raised in central Illinois, Gates now resides in San Francisco. Whenever she has a few hours of free time, she hunts for vintage jackets, walks to North Beach restaurants for risotto, creates bead-bedecked greeting cards and, of course, continues her journal writing. Gates holds a Ph.D. from the University of Illinois and has received numerous academic awards, among them Phi Beta Kappa.

LIFELINES LIBRARY ORDER FORM

FEATURING BOOKS BY GATES McKIBBIN

Book Title	Quantity	Total Cost
The Light in the Living Room: Dad's Messages from the Other Side $9.95		
LoveLines: Notes on Loving and Being Loved $9.95		
A Course in Courage: Disarming the Darkness with Strength of Heart $9.95		
A Handbook on Hope: Fusing Optimism and Action $9.95		
The Life of the Soul: The Path of Spirit in Your Lifetimes $9.95		
Available Wisdom: Insights from Beyond the Third Dimension $9.95		
Complete set of six books in the LifeLines Library $39.95		
Subtotal		
CA residents add 7.35% sales tax		
Postage and handling (F.O.B.)		
Total		

Payment Information

Charge to: VISA ☐   MasterCard   ☐

Card number _____ Exp. date_____

Ship to:

Name_____

Street_____ Apt._____

City_____ State_____ Zip_____

Phone: _____ Fax_____

E-mail: _____

To order by phone call (707) 433-9771

Fax your order to (707) 433-9772

Order via e-mail at **www.fieldflowers.com**

Visit our Website at **www.lifelineslibrary.com**

LIFELINES NOTE PADS ORDER FORM

Note Pads 12 messages in each pad, 108 pages	Quantity	Total Cost @ $7.95/pad
Authenticity (#LL1000)		
Boundaries (#LL1001)		
Change (#LL1002)		
Commitment (#LL1003)		
Companionship (#LL1004)		
Courage (#LL1005)		
Effectiveness (#LL1006)		
Hope (#LL1007)		
Love (#LL1008)		
Real Work (#LL1009)		
Strength (#LL1010)		
Time (#LL1011)		
Unconditional Love (#LL1012)		
Vitality (#LL1013)		
Wisdom (#LL1014)		
Subtotal		
CA residents add 7.35% sales tax		
Postage and handling (F.O.B.)		
Total		

Payment Information

Charge to: VISA ☐   MasterCard ☐

Card number _____ Exp. date_____

Ship to:

Name_____

Street_____ Apt._____

City_____ State_____ Zip_____

Phone: _____ Fax_____

E-mail: _____

To order by phone call (707) 433-9771

Fax your order to (707) 433-9772

Order via e-mail at **www.fieldflowers.com**

Visit our Website at **www.lifelineslibrary.com**